The Story of the Albatross

Contents

Written by Catherine Barr

Collins

1 Mythical mariners

Because a mythical Ancient Mariner made albatrosses famous

A fierce wind whipped across the weathered ship, tossing it from side to side. Freezing rain lashed across wooden decks and sailors struggled with sails. But out of this relentless storm loomed a bird so huge and magnificent that even in their plight, the sailors stopped to stare. It was called an albatross.

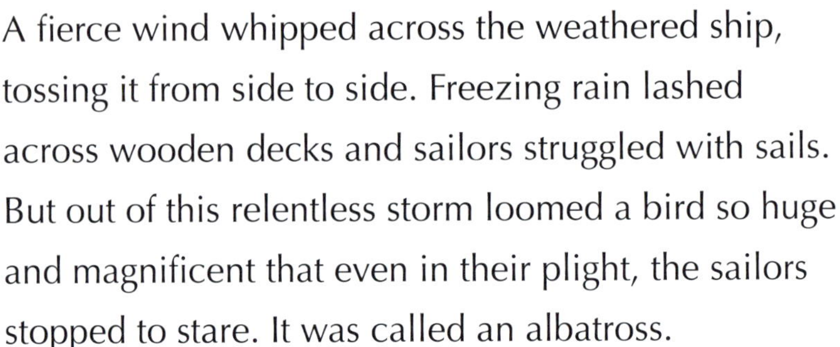

WOW!

The scientific name for the group of seabirds, including albatrosses, is Procellariiformes, from the Latin word "procella" meaning "violent storm", reflecting the stormy seas where they fly best.

This ancient story unfolds in an epic poem called "The Rime of the Ancient Mariner", published in 1798. Because of this poem, the albatross is associated with stories, storms and superstition.

H HARRAL SC

"The Rime of the Ancient Mariner" tells the story of a sailor, also known as a mariner, who shot an albatross.

The sailors are sure that killing the bird must bring bad luck. As they fear, the bad luck comes with a violent storm. But, after the storm, the wind stops and the ship is stuck. The sailors run out of water and food, and one by one they die. The only survivor is the mariner who shot the bird. Feeling full of guilt, he wanders Earth, endlessly repeating his tragic tale and wishing he had not killed the albatross.

Extract from "The Rime of the Ancient Mariner" by Samuel Taylor Coleridge

"And I had done a hellish thing,
And it would work 'em woe:
For all averred, I had killed the bird
That made the breeze to blow.
Ah wretch! said they, the bird to slay,
That made the breeze to blow!"

Wherever in the world albatrosses visit, tales of this great bird are woven into superstition, rituals and myth.

In remote seas where albatrosses live, seafarers in the past were amazed by these enormous birds. Some believed they represented the souls of sailors drowned at sea. Others thought the sight of an albatross meant a storm ahead, but if food dwindled, they shot and ate the albatrosses.

In Chile, the Yaghan people of Cape Horn wear its feathers and perform a ritual Dance of the Albatross to celebrate this magnificent bird.

In Māori tradition in New Zealand, chiefs still wear pure white albatross feathers as a symbol of peace. Their feathers are collected from albatrosses that have died, and are used to make traditional cloaks known as *korowai*.

But it was the international trade in feathers for ladies' hats worn in London and New York that pushed at least one species of albatross towards **extinction**. This trade in feathers flourished between 1870 and the 1920s. During this time, millions of short-tailed albatrosses were killed on the island of Torishima in the Pacific Ocean. Many people in Europe and North America protested against killing seabirds, eventually shutting down this trade in 1922. By then, the population of short-tailed albatrosses had plummeted, and the species was close to extinction.

2 Record breakers

Because wandering albatrosses have the longest wingspan of any flying bird

There are 22 species of albatrosses. Each species has a different shape, size and shade of white, grey and other colours that makes them distinct.

The snowy-white wandering albatross has the longest wingspan of any flying bird. From tip to tip, its record-breaking wings can be over three metres wide and carry the albatross for up to ten hours without landing.

Albatrosses use the power of the wind to help them fly. This helps them fly easily, without using much energy. As they soar, their shoulders lock so these large, heavy birds rarely need to flap their wings.

Albatrosses fly epic journeys scouring the southern oceans for food. Some even fly right around the world!

Albatrosses land on the sea to eat, to drink and to rest. But the sky is where albatrosses truly belong. For up to ten years, these enormous birds call the sky their home before finally returning to land to breed.

WOW!

One grey-headed albatross was tracked travelling the globe in just 46 days, flying an incredible 500 kilometres a day.

the migration journey of one female grey-headed albatross

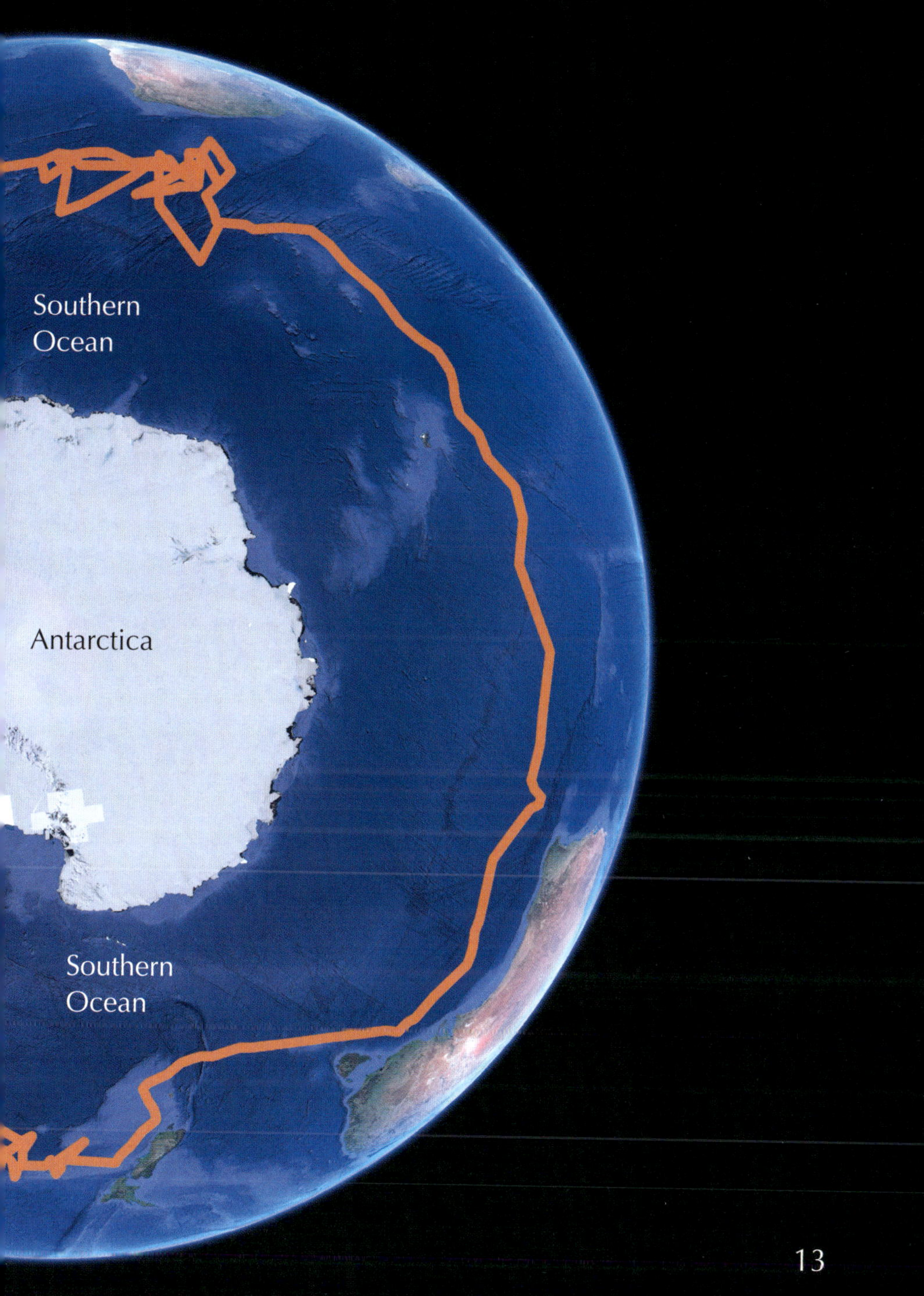
Southern
Ocean
Antarctica
Southern
Ocean

3 Faraway foragers

Because albatrosses seek food far from land on the open seas

Albatrosses look out for fish, squid and crustaceans on the surface of the sea. For easy meals, they follow fishing fleets to scavenge waste fish thrown overboard. They also snatch bait that fishers put on hooks to lure fish up from the deep.

Seabirds, including albatrosses, follow fishing boats to find fish.

Albatrosses have an incredible sense of smell. They pick up smells from 19 kilometres or more in their search for a fishy feast.

Many albatrosses prefer to eat squid rather than fish. Squid live deep in the ocean, but some of these birds have a clever way of attracting them up to the surface. They fly in tight circles at night and the spinning birds disturb **bioluminescent plankton**, which begin to glow.

When the plankton glow it lights up the ocean.

This in turn attracts squid that are hungry for plankton. As the squid reach the surface to feed, the albatrosses snap them up.

Some albatrosses fly over the warm waters of the North Pacific Ocean, and even over the equator, but most fly over the cooler southern seas. These remote, food-rich, icy waters surround Antarctica.

Penguins, whales, seabirds – such as albatrosses – and other marine life thrive in the Southern Ocean. They often feast on plankton and shrimp-like krill.

emperor penguins

krill

WOW!

Krill swarms can be so large they can be seen from space!

blue whale

4 Island hoppers

Because albatrosses choose remote ocean islands to raise their chicks

Albatrosses breed on some of the most remote islands on Earth. On these windy patches of land, they find a mate and together they raise a single chick.

More than half of the world's wandering albatrosses nest on Marion Island, part of the Prince Edward Islands – some of the only land between South Africa and Antarctica. Here, 4,500 pairs breed each year.

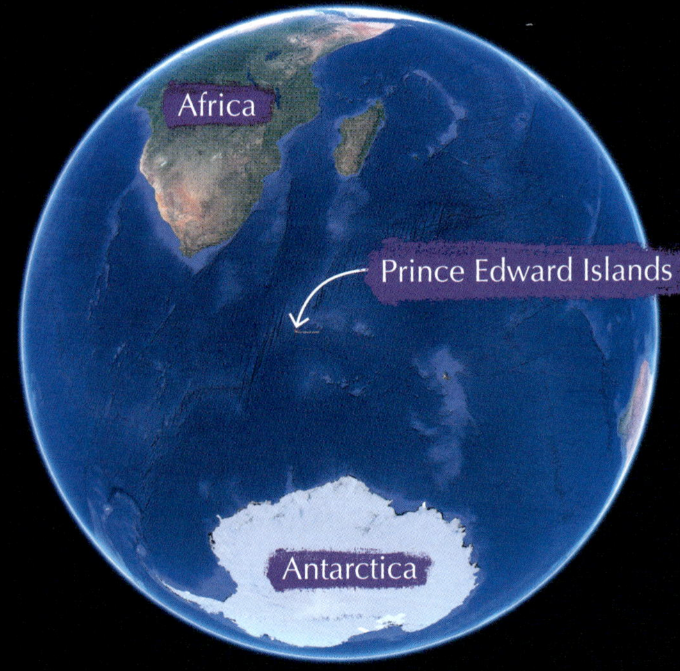

adult feeding wandering albatross chick, Marion Island, Sub-Antarctica

Albatrosses walk clumsily on land, except when they are dancing for a mate.

With gentle beak clacking, long neck swooping and body bobbing, albatrosses make a lot of effort to find and impress a potential breeding partner. They stretch up and arch their great wide wings, showing off their size and fitness. They call to the sky with clattering beaks, dancing in front of each other for an hour or more.

5 Precious egg layers

Because albatrosses lay just one big precious egg

Laying and looking after eggs and chicks uses a lot of energy. So, when they make a nest, albatrosses lay just one big egg.

WOW!

Unlike many other birds, albatrosses (and other seabirds) and hummingbirds lay oval-shaped eggs. Scientists think this is because they are high-powered flyers, so Otheir bodies create eggs that are streamlined in shape.

Some albatross species only lay an egg every two years, which is a problem if they miss a nesting season or lose an egg or chick to predators. It therefore takes a long time for populations of these extraordinary birds to recover if their numbers dip. Laying only one egg puts albatrosses at greater risk of extinction than other birds.

Adult albatrosses scrape and stick mud and grasses together to make a high-sided nest. For two or three months, albatross parents take turns to forage at sea for food, or sit on the egg, for two weeks or more at a time.

Underneath the parent's warm body as hatching approaches, it takes three days for the chick's tiny beak to peck its way out of its shell.

Once it has hatched, the pressure is on for its parents to feed this ever-hungry chick! For three weeks, albatross parents return from foraging to **regurgitate** squid, fish or krill.

By the end of the breeding season, the chick may be double the weight of their parents! This extra fat helps chicks survive during the cold winter months.

Albatross chicks have to put up with occasional storms. Smaller chicks can be blown off their nests or die from cold in strong winds, so they crouch down. A month or two after hatching, their fluff is gradually replaced by strong feathers. Finally, they are ready to be independent and take off into the wind.

Wisdom is the name given to one very specific albatross. Albatrosses can live for more than 50 years, but Wisdom is still laying eggs aged over 70 years. She is the world's oldest known wild bird.

Wisdom got her name because she's a survivor. This wise old bird has avoided fishing lines and nets, swerved predators such as sharks and plastic pollution, and is surviving the ongoing threat of **climate change**, which risks flooding her nest with rising seas.

WOW!

Wisdom has flown nearly five million kilometres to feed more than 40 chicks!

Wisdom with one of her eggs

6 Most endangered species

Because albatrosses face threats that are driving them towards extinction

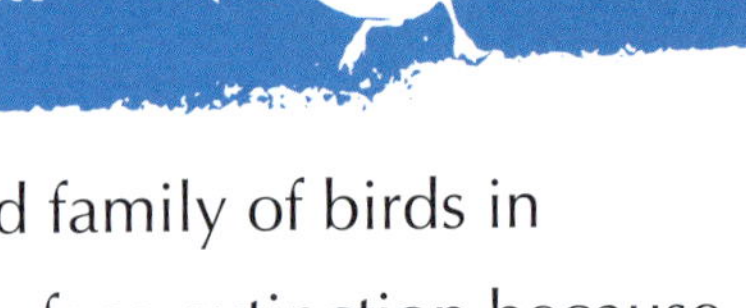

Albatrosses are the most threatened family of birds in the world. Fifteen out of 22 species face extinction because of the threats they face.

Hooks and nets

Their greatest threat is the longlines of thousands of baited fishing hooks and heavy trawling cables dragged by fishing boats. Albatrosses smell the bait, and before the hooks sink out of sight, they dive to grab the fish. Many seabirds swallow the hooks and are pulled under the waves. Longline and trawl fisheries kill hundreds of thousands of seabirds, including albatrosses, every year. This is called bycatch.

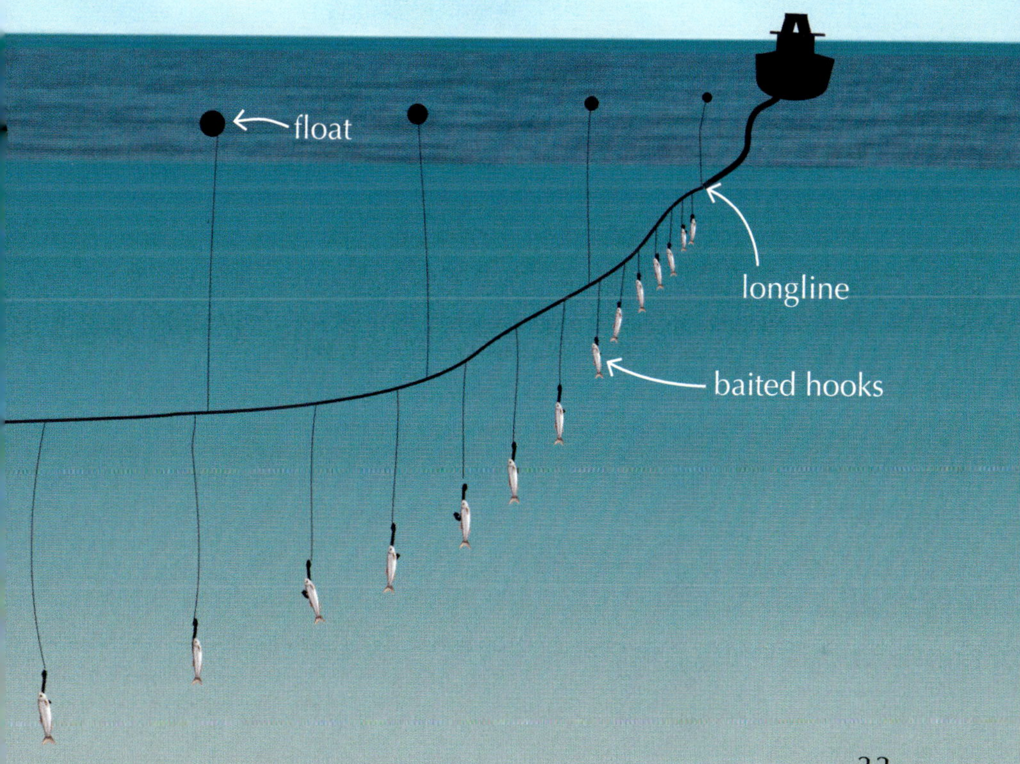

Plastic soup

Around the world, oceans swirl with plastic that has been thrown into it rather than being recycled correctly.. Albatrosses can choke on floating plastic that they mistake for food and, tragically, they often feed it to their chicks when they return to the nest.

Less food

Warmer waters are less productive, so as climate change warms the southern ocean, albatrosses may have to fly further to find enough food for their chicks. As humans take ever more fish out of the sea, albatrosses and other seabirds face even bigger challenges to find enough food and survive.

Mouse attack!

Ocean islands are naturally free of predators like mice, rats and cats. But hundreds of years ago these creatures crept onto or were taken aboard ships. They escaped and settled on new island homes where seabirds such as albatrosses nest.

These new inhabitants upset the balance of nature on islands where birds had not **evolved** to escape predators. For example, mice climb into their nests to eat the eggs and attack chicks. This causes huge losses in the number of albatrosses surviving to become adult birds.

Work is being done to remove these predators from albatross nesting sites to protect the eggs and babies.

5

7 Spectacular survivors

Because there is hope for the survival of albatrosses

Due to the threats they face, and with each pair having one chick every one or two years, albatrosses are disappearing. The Albatross Task Force was formed by two organisations that specialise in protecting birds. The job of the Task Force's experts is to work alongside fishers on boats to find ways to fish without killing seabirds.

Off the coast of Namibia in southern Africa, there has been incredible success, where the deaths of albatrosses in fisheries have been reduced by 99%. Here are some of the ways they are helping to save them:

Weighted hooks: The baited fishing hooks have heavier weights attached to them, so they sink more quickly. Surface-feeding birds don't get the chance to snack.

Night setting: Putting out longlines at night helps save seabirds that only feed in daylight.

Bird scaring or "tori" lines: Brightly coloured ropes with streamers towed behind fishing boats scare birds away from baited hooks. In Namibia, these rainbow ropes are handmade by local communities.

Bright "tori lines" scare the birds away from the baited hooks on the longlines.

8 Returning storytellers

Because tracked albatrosses return year after year

Many albatrosses are now fitted with electronic tags to track their epic journeys. Scientists use information from the tags to find the fisheries that are the greatest threat to the birds. They can then plan how to protect seabirds from the risks they face.

Accelerometers count the number of times the bird has flapped its wings. Scientists can then learn how albatrosses fly in different winds. This helps them work out how climate change might impact the albatrosses' survival in more extreme weather.

fitting an albatross with a satellite tracking device

researchers checking Laysan and black-footed albatrosses and their chicks

Since albatrosses nest on remote ocean islands, scientists have to make long boat rides in person to reach the birds' nests to carefully and very gently attach tags to them.

The tags map the flight paths and extraordinary, record-breaking journeys. Albatrosses return to the same island again and again, so scientists are able to follow the stories of the same birds year after year.

Albatrosses are an important part of ocean ecosystems. Yet the survival of these huge birds is seriously threatened. Human activities such as fishing, pollution and climate change have pushed them to the edge of extinction.

Today, scientists are monitoring and protecting albatrosses around the world. The good news is that in places where fisheries, their greatest threat, take action to avoid catching seabirds, there is huge success. If countries and communities work together, albatrosses can be free to forever cruise the wild oceans where they belong.

Glossary

bioluminescent plankton tiny sea creatures that light up when disturbed by movement or predators

climate change changes in world weather, most recently caused by human activities such as burning fossil fuels

evolved changed and developed over time

extinction living things that have died out and no longer exist

regurgitate to bring up food stored in a bird's stomach to feed chicks

Index

Albatross threats

Threats	
swallowing baited fishing hooks	
climate change making it harder to find food	
plastic pollution being eaten by birds	
eggs and chicks being eaten by predators such as mice, rats and cats	

Solutions

coloured streamer lines, heavier weights and fishing at night

tagging and monitoring the birds

recycling plastic and avoiding littering

removal of mice, rats and cats from albatross nesting sites

Ideas for reading

Written by Gill Matthews
Primary Literacy Consultant

Reading objectives:

- read books that are structured in different ways and reading for a range of purposes
- use dictionaries to check the meaning of words that they have read
- check that the text makes sense to them, discuss their understanding and explaining the meaning of words in context
- ask questions to improve their understanding of a text
- retrieve and record information from non-fiction

Spoken language objectives:

- ask relevant questions to extend their understanding and knowledge
- use relevant strategies to build their vocabulary
- articulate and justify answers, arguments and opinions

Curriculum links: Science: living things and their habitats

Interest words: whipped, lashed, loomed, flourished, plummeted

Resources: dictionary

Build a context for reading

- Ask children to look at the front cover and to read the title. Explore what they already know about albatrosses, or their impression of the bird from the cover image.
- Read the back-cover blurb. Discuss what threats children think might be facing albatrosses.
- Point out that this is an information book. Ask children what they know about non-fiction and what features they expect to find in the book.
- Ask them to find in the book some of the features they have mentioned. Discuss the purpose and organisation of a contents page, glossary and index.
- Ask children to use the contents page to find the chapter called *Mythical mariners*.

Understand and apply reading strategies

- Read pp2–9 aloud. Ask children to summarise the information in this chapter.